groundswell mixtape copyright 2014

TABLE OF CONTENTS

Groundswell: Oral History for Social Change is a network of oral historians, activists, cultural workers, community organizers, and documentary artists that use oral history to further movement building and transformative social change.

Our network grew out of an initial in-person Gathering of 15 activist oral historians in the fall of 2011. Today, the Groundswell network includes hundreds of individuals from all across the United States, as well as from other countries.

Our Mission: We believe that oral history can be a source of power, knowledge and strength in our struggles for justice. Oral history provides a unique space for those most impacted by injustice to speak and be heard in their own voices. Groundswell's mission is to provide mutual support, training, and resources in the practice of applied community-based history in order to build the creativity and power of social justice movements.

In seeking to create a supportive community, we welcome practitioners of all skill levels and backgrounds. We believe that oral history is both an art and a skill demanding thoughtfulness, preparation, research, training, practice and a high degree of integrity and follow-through. We promote high standards of quality and celebrate the many forms in which movement-relevant oral history and storytelling work happens.

MixTape is a project from our second Gathering in the spring of 2013 that shares the work of some of these groups.

If you would like to join our growing community please see our website, www.oralhistoryforsocialchange.org, to learn more about us.

ALISA DEL TUFO

Threshold Collaborative
www.thresholdcollaborative.org

Threshold Collaborative uses story as a catalyst for change. Our methods are designed to deepen empathy and ignite action in order to build more just, caring, and healthy communities. We have developed a set of participatory strategies and human-centered design. These integrate "engaged storytelling," photography, and video to document, explore, and learn about issues from the perspective of "resident experts"— the people living, working, and going to school in our communities. By sharing stories, insights, and ideas, the people most impacted and often marginalized contribute to change that promotes equity and justice. Our work builds inclusion, democratizes knowledge, and finds sustainable solutions to challenges.

We work with individuals, organizations, and communities interested in igniting, building, strengthening, and sustaining social change and justice efforts. Our works spans issues and geography as we partner with groups all over the country to help them integrate the power of story into their work.

We want to surface the experiences, insights, and feelings of people at the margins, bringing their voice and reality into efforts to build a more just and caring world.

At Threshold we:
- Teach and coach you and your constituents to share stories and surface their ideas and experiences through a series of workshops and engagements tailored to your needs
- Develop community engagement, participatory research, story gathering, communication strategies, and campaigns
- Produce dynamic, multimedia content that tell the stories that matter to your community
- Design artful, creative, powerful, and effective ways to share the stories that matter with broad and diverse audiences

Threshold focuses primarily on audio recording shared in tandem with photography. We have a variety of artful and creative ways to share this work in public and intimate settings.

The WRI Oral History Project
wri-voices.org

The WRI Oral History Project documents the history of the Welfare Rights Initiative (WRI), a grassroots student activist and community leadership training organization located at Hunter College. The aim is to examine, via these oral history interviews, social movement activity at the level of a grassroots organization as exemplified by the WRI. WRI was developed to aid student welfare recipients to become agents of social change and actively involve them with policymaking.

This project documents WRI's progression from a student- and faculty-led grassroots movement to its present incarnation as a student advocacy organization. WRI seeks to serve underserved populations citywide, primarily women and girls, via its outreach programs that are designed to encourage those who are economically disadvantaged to study and obtain higher education and/ or job training.

This oral history project gives a platform to those who generally

Former and/or current welfare recipients—WRI's founders and membership base. It will also provide students and scholars of social movements with a positive working example of how women from various backgrounds can band together and enact social change.

One important element in this project has been to emphasize that WRI is a Community-Based Archive. In the context of community-based archiving and its demand that we all acknowledge the reality of growing disparities in the historical record and their social consequences. An inability to access scholarship is a symptom of a much larger issue. For WRI, inaccesibility is recognized as a troubling component within a larger network of socioeconomic factors that include the inequities and systematic impoverishment of the public education system and the "disruption" of higher education. We have unprecedented need for this type of scholarship to be widely and freely available. Providing a web-based portal for WRI's story was a key element in addressing this problem, and this principle provides the foundational basis for this project.

The hope is that participation in oral histories by WRI alumni, students, and leaders' will encourage the active use of their stories in scholarship, activism, and policymaking. Through digital technologies such as social media and semantic web markup, which have been incorporated in each individual interview record in the archive, will increase the discoverability of these interviews with an underrepresented portion in the community, and presents a more vital role in framing the historical record.

have little voice in the public debate on welfare reform.

AMY HILL

Silence Speaks: Storytelling and Participatory Media for Human Rights Promotion
www.silencespeaks.org

Silence Speaks (www.silencespeaks.org) aims to situate first-person audio and visual narratives of people directly affected by human rights abuses as key ingredients of human rights work. As a project of the Center for Digital Storytelling (www.storycenter.org), we use participatory media, popular education, and testimonio practices to support the telling and witnessing of stories that all too often remain unspoken and unheard—stories of struggle, courage, and transformation. With the permission of storytellers and project partners, stories created through our processes are shared in local communities and globally through broadcast or social media outlets, as strategic tools for training, grassroots organizing, and policy advocacy to promote dignity, long-term change, and justice.

We work in close partnership with other nonprofits/NGOs and grassroots groups in the United States and around the world to support their constituents in sharing stories and demanding to be heard. Since our beginnings in 1999, we have led more than 35 projects in locations across the United States and in Australia, Belize, Brazil, Canada, Republic of Congo (Congo-Brazzaville), Guatemala, Nepal, South Africa, and Uganda to surface narratives by women and men affected by and advocating against gender-based violence; unfair treatment of labor migrants, women survivors of war, and young people formerly associated with fighting forces; child sexual abuse; the lack of adolescent-appropriate programs and policies to support sexual health and rights; and more. In all of our projects, we focus on storytelling by those most vulnerable to human rights abuses—young people; the poor; indigenous groups; women; survivors of conflict; LGBTQ individuals; etc.

Our projects employ a unique blend of testimonio and autobiographical writing methods, participatory media approaches such as digital storytelling and Photovoice, and interactive group processes to assist storytellers in reflecting on their lives, identifying meaningful stories, and crafting their narratives into short, powerful audiovisual pieces. Above all, our work is guided by careful attention to the ethics of bringing sensitive personal narratives into public spheres.

As a participatory media program, technology is key to our work, yet, technology does not drive our work. We use those tools deemed most appropriate through careful consultation with our partners working on the ground. Where possible, storytellers learn the skills for editing their own short videos. In other cases, when intensive skill-building is either not relevant or not desired, we focus on simpler technologies like still photography. Specific outputs for stories are determined in collaboration with partners and can include

- Web and social-media-ready videos
- Customized web presentations
- Story collections on playable DVD
- Radio productions integrating stories
- Print publications, posters, or billboards
- Story-based discussion guides and curricular materials

RECLAIMING OURSELVES

Black Women's Blueprint, Inc. is a civil and human rights organization of women and men.

Our purpose is to take immediate action to secure social, political and economic equality in American society. We work to develop a culture where women of African descent are fully empowered and where gender, race and other disparities are erased. We engage in progressive research, historical documentation, support movement building and organize on social justice issues steeped in the struggles of Black women within their communities and within dominant culture.

FARAH TANIS

www.blackwomensblueprint.org

The essence of Black Women's Blueprint is to deploy our voices in the wars against sexual assault, shatter the silence that prevails and the almost complete invisibility within our Black communities and in greater society about Black women's lives, about the level of sexual violence, and the systematic exclusion of our specific gendered experiences in the broader agenda for racial justice and human rights.www.blackwomensblueprint.org

Our objectives are to develop a national collection and video/audio recordings of oral history and narratives from over 10,000 Black/African-American survivors of rape (age 15-85) in six U.S. locations, and provide a public record of the impact of rape on their lives and their specific demands for particular resources in their own words.

Black Women's Blueprint uses combination of one on one interviews using audio and video recording tools, a telephone message line and emailed stories. We are also using theater to tell stories, and via our Museum, The Museum of Women's Resistance, is curating exhibits using art to relay oral narratives. The Museum of Women's Resistance was recently recognized as a Site of Conscience.

POLK

Polk Street: Lives in Transition

JOEY PLASTER

jplaster.commons.yale.edu/polk-street-lives-in-transition

Awarded the American Historical Association's 2010 Allan Berube Prize for public humanities, Polk Street: Lives in Transition interpreted more than seventy original oral histories in relation to contemporary neighborhood change and conflict.

San Francisco's Polk Street had long been a national destination and home to some of the most underrepresented persons of the LGBT community, including homeless youth, immigrants, and trans women. From 2007-2009, with the area's remaining gay and trans bars closing, rising rents forcing out long-time residents, and middle-income businesses, restaurants, bars, and residents quickly moving in, this public humanities project sought to build bridges and facilitate dialog through a number of venues:

- A traveling multimedia exhibit
- A series of professionally mediated neighborhood dialogues
- Oral history "listening parties"
- Historical narrative commissioned by the Center for Lesbian and Gay Studies at CUNY
- "Polk Street Stories" radio docu produced with Jay Allison and distributed nationally via NPR

We work with non-profits, business associations, and long-time residents. The project was designed to build bridges between different community members.

www.transoralhistory.com

The Transgender Oral History Project (TOHP) is a community-driven effort to collect, preserve, and share a diverse range of stories from within transgender and gender variant communities.

We fight the oppression of trans people by documenting lived experiences, teaching media production skills, and facilitating grassroots media projects.

The TOHP is dedicated to creating media that:

- Represents trans people as agents of change
- Reframes the challenges trans people face in structural terms
- Challenges patriarchal constructions of gender
- Empowers subjects through engaging them in the production process
- Centers the lived experience of trans people of color, immigrants, and other trans people who are underrepresented in mainstream media

Mainstream media narratives treat transgender people as oddities, probe individuals about their bodily choices, and directly reinforce harmful stereotypes. These stories frame trans issues around individualized problems—obscuring the ways that patriarchy, racism, and other forms of oppression impact our lives—and therefore elude the need for social change, ally support, and policy reform. We intervene in this hostile climate with media created to empower our community, to engage our allies and activists, and to redefine oppressive narratives.

The audience for our project is twofold: we seek to reach trans, gender variant, and questioning people because we want to portray positive role models, decrease isolation, foster a sense of shared history, and build community among trans people of different backgrounds. We also seek to educate the general public about the diversity of trans experiences. By recording and disseminating our stories, we challenge the oppressive narratives that dominate mainstream media portrayals of trans people.

Founded in 2008 as a national network, we operate through local working groups based in Philadelphia and Chicago. In the past five years, we have interviewed forty-seven trans people in twelve states, led interactive workshops at conferences and community centers across the country, and created installations in gallery and university spaces. We strive to increase the reach of this work through community education efforts such as workshops, lectures, and screenings. Fee-for-service work at larger institutions like colleges and universities allows us to reach smaller, community-based organizations that could not otherwise fund us to travel. Right now we are working on a Youth Educators Toolkit, which contains short documentaries paired with lesson plans that allow youth groups and educators to educate themselves and others about trans issues. Our first toolkit, scheduled for release this winter, focuses on media literacy, employment, and healthcare.

In order to make our work accessible beyond those spaces we can physically reach, we've also built an online story bank, founded a zine distro to disseminate self-published works by transgender authors, and published the stories shared through our project in both print and multimedia forms.

15

SUZY SUBWAYS

slamherstory.wordpress.com

The SLAM! Herstory Project is a growing multimedia oral history of the Student Liberation Action Movement (SLAM!), a multiracial, radical student activist group at the City University of New York (CUNY) from 1996 to 2007. Origininating with the CUNY Coalition Against the Cuts in 1995. The blog features archival documents, photos, analytical writing, edited excerpts of interview transcripts, audio clips from interviews, audio and video recordings of speaking events, and videos edited by SLAM! members for the group's tenth anniversary in 2006. Three former SLAM! members, who have been trained in oral history methodology as part of the project, are now recording radio-quality audio interviews with former SLAM! and CUNY Coalition members. Audio clips from these interviews will be up on the site soon.

The SLAM! Herstory Project aims to offer current and future students and radical organizers collaboratively sourced political theory in the voices and with the stories of those who tried it out in practice. We work with current CUNY student organizers to plan events and share lessons learned from our history.

The blog is a work in progress, building toward a well-organized archive of oral history interview audio segments. A fully developed website will make the audio clips more accessible to students and radicals everywhere. Unedited audio interviews and transcripts will be donated to the SLAM! collection at the Tamiment Library at New York University. Interview segments will be edited into a book-length oral narrative by the coordinator of the interviewing project, with feedback from collaborative listening sessions where narrators will discuss what needs to be included. A speaking tour featuring narrators and interviewers will promote the website and book at universities and activist organizing spaces around the country.

"Our aim is to support neighbors and friends in their efforts to sustain a vibrant, equitable community based in part on the example of leadership and creative service regaled in oral histories."

DELLA POLLOCK

The Jackson Center for Making and Saving History
www.jacksoncenter.info

The Jackson Center for Saving and Making History is an oral history and organizing hub for civil rights education, youth development, and housing justice in the Chapel Hill/Carrboro area.

- We honor, preserve, and engage civil rights and local history, bringing the history of struggle into active consciousness, dialogue, and action.

- We facilitate community-first housing processes and deep neighborhood networks that utilize our internal power to educate and sustain our communities.

- We organize a nationally recognized youth-owned radio program, a resident-driven newspaper, an oral history trust, and other civic media outlets that honor and amplify voices for social change from within.

In so doing:

- We challenge historical amnesia of a "progressive town" by honoring civil rights history and bringing the history of struggle into active consciousness, dialogue, and action for continued policy transformation.

- We challenge predatory housing practices through our community-first housing processes and deep neighborhood networks that utilize our internal power to educate and sustain our communities.

- We challenge media bias and discrimination by hosting alternative youth-led radio, resident-driven newspaper, our oral history trust, and other civic media outlets that honor and amplify voices for change from within.

Located at the gateway to the formerly segregated neighborhoods of the university town of Chapel Hill, North Carolina, the center's work has grown out of and is committed to engaging difference. We work across all preconceived boundaries of division in the area, including race, class, religion, sexuality, and education. Our primary collaborators have a sustained commitment to community and social justice.

Many participants are low-wealth residents, with four and five-generation histories in the area; some living in limited public housing. We are engaged in fighting the drive to high-wealth homogeneity in a town increasingly dependent on low-wage workers, the majority of whom live 10-30 miles away from university and town work sites.

JOHN CHOE

One Flushing Community Economic Development Center
www.oneflushing.org

ONE FLUSHING is a community development center that seeks to build a strong, diverse, and sustainable Flushing community by expanding economic opportunities and prosperity for all. One strategy we employ is to document and share the amazing stories of those who live and work in Flushing, New York, through our "Voices of Flushing" oral history project. "Voices of Flushing" seeks to encourage greater dialogue, understanding, and solidarity across race, ethnicity, religion, and culture. The stories highlight the rich diversity found in Flushing as well as the common ground we need to help us move forward.

One Flushing's oral history project seeks to tell the stories of the people who live and work in Flushing. In our 2012 survey, we contacted over a thousand local businesses, nonprofit organizations, cultural centers, and houses of worship. We went back and interviewed some of the small business owners, residents, and civic and religious leaders for our "Voice of Flushing" project to begin to document their stories in greater depth. These are the community members we seek to bring together and help through our technical assistance, research, and advocacy.

The goal of "Voices of Flushing" is to document and share the amazing stories of those who live and work in Flushing. We hope to encourage greater dialogue, understanding and solidarity across race, ethnicity, religion, and culture. By highlighting our unique and rich diversity, we seek common ground to help us move forward.

We have worked with the Columbia University Oral History Masters Program to document stories using both audio and video interviews. We have been editing and distributing selected clips from each interview via YouTube and social media. We not only hope to increase mutual understanding and solidarity in our diverse community, but also showcase and promote the small business owners, civic leaders, and community members who make up Flushing.

We are documenting the stories with video and audio files that we edit and distribute via YouTube and social media (including Facebook). We hope to use other media (long-form video documentary) as well as activities (exhibits, forums, film screenings, etc.) to share and facilitate dialogue in the Flushing community.

the Neighborhood Story Project

ABRAM HIMELSTEIN

Neighborhood Story Project- New Orleans, Louisiana
www.neighborhoodstoryproject.org

Before and after the cameras and microphones come and take our images and tell our stories, the Neighborhood Story Project is at work in collaborative ethnography. Creative non-fiction, writing workshops, oral histories, and photography lead to books and posters. We celebrate the release of our publications with parties- and royalties come back to community members who write the books.

We began in a public high school the year before Katrina, and have created more than 40 books and posters that are venerated city-wide and used in high school and college classrooms around the country.

www.workingnarratives.org

WORKING NARRATIVES works with movements to tell great stories that inspire, activate and enliven our democracy. We believe that social movements thrive and win when they draw on participants' personal experiences and local cultures. By telling stories—whether in the form of performance, radio, video, or other media—movements build power, envision new democratic possibilities, and change culture and policy. Our work is located at the intersection of arts, technology, and policy. We work with grassroots groups, media-makers, artists, and foundations.

Our two main projects now are:

NATION INSIDE: A network that connects and supports people who are building a movement to systematically challenge mass incarceration in the United States. We offer grassroots groups training in how to tell and deploy stories; technology to produce and disseminate stories (including clip-cams, a 1-800 storyline, and a web platform for partner campaigns); and networking to build power in the movement against mass incarceration.

"**STORYTELLING AND SOCIAL CHANGE**": A strategy guide primarily for funders, but also for activists, storytellers, and media-makers of all sorts. The guide looks at the recent history of storytelling and social change; reviews the theories of change behind this work; provides case studies of 10 projects and their funders; offers guidance on every stage of grantmaking; includes sidebar interviews and other features; and lists resources for additional exploration.

We welcome your input and participation in any of our projects.

SARAH LOOSE

Roots and Wings Project
www.rop.org

Roots & Wings: The Past and Future of Rural Oregon's Grassroots Movement for Human Dignity is a participatory oral history project to document and learn from the Rural Organizing Project's (ROP) 20-year history of progressive organizing in rural and small town Oregon.

The project seeks to critically analyze and articulate what's at the heart of ROP's organizing model through the voices, stories and reflections of historic and current ROP members, volunteers, staff, board, allies and critics. What's worked? What hasn't? What's unique about what we do? And what does it all mean for our organizing moving forward?

roots & wings

RURAL ORGANIZING PROJECT

18 Years of Advancing Democracy in Rural Oregon

25

We work with over 60 Human Dignity Groups (HDGs) which make up the ROP network. These HDGs, powered by hundreds of volunteers, organize for immigrant rights, LGBTQ rights, & economic and racial justice in communities across the state. ROP serves as a critical link and catalyst to this network. It supports the formation of new HDGs and builds the power and capacity of existing groups. The Roots & Wings Oral History Project aims to share ROP's history and model with ROP/HDG leaders and members, as well as people in other states looking to learn more about how to do grassroots organizing in conservative and rural settings.

With the Roots & Wings Oral History Project, we hope to document and share ROP's institutional memory, history, and organizing model. But we also aim to improve our practice and inform our future organizing plans. By exploring ROP's history through the stories of those who have created it and been changed because of it, we can learn something about the power and potential of rural organizing. We can begin to uncover a counter narrative to the dominant story of rural Oregon. And, with a critical look at our own history, we can better understand what it means—and what it takes—to do grassroots, values-driven, progressive organizing in rural communities.

Our strategies include:

- Recording oral history interviews with historic and current ROP/HDG activists, leaders, staff, board, and allies. We create a detailed log for each interview (though not a full transcript).

- Facilitating workshops where ROP members and leaders have the opportunity to listen to and reflect on interview excerpts, ROP archives, and their own experience. (These have been done in conjunction with a 5-year strategic planning process.)

- Creating an organizer-friendly booklet (and expanded online version) that uses essays, interview excerpts and archives to share and analyze ROP's organizing model, history and lessons learned.

www.ingramcontent.com/pod-product-compliance
Lightning Source LLC
Chambersburg PA
CBHW041827280526
45792CB00006B/2018